Bronze and

C000254174

Vaibhavi Pandey

Cover by Arya Pandey
Illustrated by Arya Pandey and Janhavi Kolte

ISBN:9798354782239

DEDICATION

To the woods and the sky, that have continually inspired me, but most importantly, to Dadi (Mrs. Sarla Pandey) and Nani (Late Mrs. Vimla Pandey), whose unending love made me believe I could love myself too. This is for you.

Bronze and Mahogany

CONTENTS

Bronze and Mahogany

ACKNOWLEDGMENTS

I am deeply indebted to the following people, without whom this book would not have been possible. My English teacher Mrs. Karuna Malhotra, who first gave me the inspiration to write poetry and made it seem like my voice mattered too. My dad, who patiently listened to my cliché poems in 6th grade and yet seemed to always have words of appreciation. Without you and your push to publish this book, I wouldn't have the courage to make this happen. Mumma, your quiet support has oftentimes said more than anyone's words could have. Thank you for your faith in me. Thank you to my beautiful little sister Vagmi, who has gotten me through these 5 years with all her love. Whenever you're old enough to read this, know that you'll go places, and never let anyone tell you otherwise. Didi is so grateful to have you in her life. My grandparents Dadi (Mrs. Sarla Pandey), Baba (Mr. Harishyam Pandey), Nani (Late Mrs. Vimla Pandey) and Nana (Late Mr. VN Pandey), who with their endless selflessness and resilience have given me the values that I most prize, and I strive to live up to the intentions they set for me every single day. Thank you so much Chachi, Chacha and Aadi, for giving me some of my happiest memories that often ended up becoming my inspiration to write. Kritika, for always having critiqued my work in the best possible way, appreciating it profoundly and cringing sincerely when appropriate. I have come to trust your writer's instinct perhaps even more than mine. Thank you for being my happy place, bestie! To Aroo bhaiya, for being the coolest cousin ever, and doing the brilliant illustrations and cover of this book for me, along with Janhavi Kolte, the designer that awed me beyond comprehension with her work. Both of you alongside your very busy freshman year at NID have taken the time & made this book come to life in better ways than I could have expected. I cannot thank you enough. And finally, thank you, dear reader, for giving me your most precious possession – your time. I hope I make it worth your while.

Bronze and Mahogany

16

SALTWATER

Yet another day, saltwater drips down
Slowly and slowly, and yet a huge wave
The ocean rises higher
And I tell myself, "Just keep swimming"
When will the tide go out?

I'm swimming, I'm swimming
I'm drowning, I'm drowning
They've tied bricks to my ankles
And all I can tell myself, "Just keep swimming"

It's raging, it's raging
The storm, it scares me
My lungs feel the saltwater in them, overpowering
Snatching my breath,
Clutching my tender hope in its claws
Seizing my sanity in its bones

How strange, what came from me,
My own,
The saltwater that I bled
Cutting me open and making me tumble
Right down in the depths of its blue
When will I reach the shore?

OCEANS

Oh, but look! An ocean born
So tranquil, so at peace
With placidity it is adorned
So untroubled, so at ease

And oh but look! Look at it grow,
The tides and the storms
It seems so long, oh ages ago
When she was her primitive form

But why is she now so suddenly still
Where is the clamor that she prized?
Oh Lord, she seems startlingly ill
But her tears flow in disguise

Oh but look, ages it's been
She's seen her highs and lows,
Yet she adores her clamant, quiet skin
And tells everyone she knows:

"Beware! There will be storms and tides,
Remain calm as life unfurls,
The waters birth their struggles,
As will they birth pearls!"

SMILES

Echoes, echoes of their footsteps
Drowned by the crippling color
The sunlight blinds me
As this salt, this water runs down my skin
Tumbling from the blues in my eye

The torso of air hugging me,
Half-sung hymns and a heart rusted black
These limbs walk down sidewalks
Pavements built over shadows and bones never buried

Cracked lips smile smiles
Testament to a triumph that's never been known
But are they smiles, are they tears of joy,
Or perhaps not?

LIGHT AND SHADOW

"Will the hollow of the night
Really bleed into the day?
Will the dawn as red as cherry
Really rise from faraway?

Will the nether reaches of shadow
Ever let the light escape?
Oh when shall the morning's view
Come brightly into shape?"

"Not you worry, simple friend,
For there is another sky
And while the black is raging,
The white so tranquil lie

Never mind the icy forests
Nor bother their damp twins
For there blooms another garden
Where not a frost has been

Never hail, the bees hum,
And every corner leaks the same sound,
"Shadow is proof that light's behind you,
All you must do is turn around!"

Tears

The fire in these veins
Kindled, and raged, and now lies quiet
Sleeping, dormant

The smoke on these lips
Burned, and flew, and now lies quiet
Nothing but a black residue

Blood stains these fists
That once tasted of anger and vengeance, and now lies tired
Exhausted, drained

What did I fight for?
Why must I fail?
Why must these jaded, and worn, and frayed
And scruffy, derelict tears slip through

Why must their waterfall be a beautiful creation,
That tourists come to watch,
Park their cars and stand
And encapsulate the memory
Of watching me drown in my own waters

Continued… Page 21

Bronze and Mahogany

And yet I wish, this cavern was dewy still
That my river hadn't run dry
Even though it has
And run its course, oh how it ran
Ran, and ran, and ran till it was gasping

"Tears - the blood of the soul"

And if they're true,
Those words I read,
Oh how I bled,
Oh how I bled

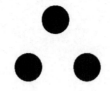

1,2,3

Watch me
Watch me as I pirouette through the echoes of your voice
Watch me as I pivot to the music of all the pretty little lies you
told me
Watch my pas-de-bourrée as I blur all those fights and all those
taunts
As I spin and all I can think of is the music
How we waltzed - 1,2,3
1,2,3
1,2,3
The lights - changing and shifting- black and white,
black and white,
shadow and light,
Look at this wreck, this mess, these ruins of my sanity
Wave your hands through the debris
And look at the destruction you've caused
And yet,
and yet
If I could do it all again, I would
I would rather drown in your darkness again
than swim in someone else's light.

TIME

Infinities, infinities
Of time and space
Reminding me of each second that is
Rushing, dashing, shooting

Perpetual, incessant, impatient
Oh, time!
How agitated, how restless
How eager you are, to leave me behind

Sprinting, fleeing, breathless
And yet seemingly a placid lake
A tranquil scenery to calm one down
What flawless facade, time!

How pretentious you are, what a performer
Doubling, tripling, quadrupling your pace each second
Watching, smirking, as I lose you, lose myself
And yet I am growing, bursting, blooming, falling

My capabilities erupting with each step you take
Boundless,
And yet I can't help but detest you for running
For leaving

Alas,
Infinities, infinities.

HAZEL

Broken ties, your hazel eyes
The tender stroke of time, blowing with the wind
Shards of glass, severed and weak
You and I, a little peek
Into the past
A mirage
Happiness is an illusion
But your caramel voice, your honey eyes
We're in a field of sugarcanes
Then why does the air taste bitter?

Oh, cut me loose, set me free
Erase all my memories
Freeze the moments
The grains of sand in our hands
Lying in the sun, lying to them

Tell me and I'll turn the car back around
Take me back to the wreckage and the ruins
Walk through the rubble of our yesterdays
Tell me, and I'll wind the clock back to us

But now we're back
To your silence, to your choice
Perhaps not the first time, but the second, the third, the
thousandth?

AUTUMN

Fickle minds, crippled signs
I feel my breath,
Rising, Falling
Bite my tongue,
Is the night over yet?

Scraped knees and shredded trees
Autumn came too early
Unwelcoming womb to static tomb
Bazaars that hum and buzz like bees

I see, I touch, I feel

I'm sorry
That you were so cold, and I cackled with fire
That you couldn't drown me with your noise
For minus and minus don't really make plus

Polaroid magazines and shower curtains
Cushion covers and white roses
Carpeted floors to banging doors

I'm sorry
That I couldn't contain your frigid within me
For autumn came too early
Unwelcoming womb,
Classic doom.

SUNSHINE

Frenzied crowds and busy streets
Hustle culture, little sleep
He was my sunshine,
When did I burn me in his gaze?

Violent sunshine, curious creature
Desolate wind and howling aims
We were running and out of breath
Was our birth just our death?

"A pretty Cryer"
Soaked in my tears - they call me pretty
For beauty trumps pain

For I must be burning alive
And all they could feel was the warmth on their skin,
Blind to my ashes
Deaf to my screams

Agony, agony
Squandered love
Tape me up and piece me together

They swim in the blood, but don't see the blade
It killed me to love him, so I buried my grave
He was my sunshine, but I forgot the shade.

TYPEWRITER

Rusted typewriter, my finger's muse
"Argumentative", his ego bruised
Neon signs, lemon ice
Cease the fire already

Shoelaces tight, it feels just right
So used to the running
Breath leveled, overused pedal
So used to the running

Each drop of blood accounted for,
We were ravens in the night, eagles in flight
Rainkissed mud that put us to sleep
Predator to prey, heaven's sheep

Devious pawns, we were pigs for slaughter
My hateful gaze and your sorry face
Corks off, the champaign flew

Now here we are in this wretched maze
Calloused fingers, our love ablaze
Cracked corners and paper cuts
Easy madness, simple craze

Bloodshed, war, fighting, peace
Red and blue and willow green
And always, I come sprinting back
To this rusted typewriter, painted black
With paper cuts that never quite heal.

Riptide

Eyes open, eyes closed
Anticipating the riptide
Pull me in close

Sinners and givers
Easy hate, changing with the tides
Contain my fire, deny my truth
Frantic music, our 'wild' youth

For there are secrets buried in these chaste walls
Echoes and kaleidoscopic visions
Colored in by your open flight
Bronze and mahogany and copper dreams
Dented and bended and crumpled

Where did it all go?
Reaching for, but never quite reaching there,
Arrows strike,
Mock my quiet and tame my roar

And the stain faded, but so did the color
Fakers and takers
Uneasy love, eternal divides
This wave of unsaid words,
And I drowned.

KISS

What a summer
Chromatic and ripe
Your regard, sardonic and superior
My eyes, stunted and downcast
How,
How did you make me guilty of a forgotten crime?

Tarnished summer
Ashes in the air
My young bones, worn with time
Broken, patched, haunting, dashed
You drove a stake through me, and somehow screamed in agony?

Snap me out of this daze
As the mirrors shatter
"A knife cuts both ways", how fake
You, and your ruby eyes
Swell with pride but red with rage

You put me on a pedestal, and I fell
Take me to the paddy mazes
Sink my feet in their blue
Take me to the northern lights
With their southern skies
And their pretty lies
My quick demise
Oh, so unwise

Continued… Page 39

And now the smoke lifts
Disgruntled and double faced, you
With your entourage of mortal sins
Cynical and grappling
At the feet of my throne
Built with the stones you threw at me
What an exquisite honor
Sorrow and bliss,
Hell's kiss.

ENOUGH

Are the sunsets any different?
How are the stars that you left us for?
Are you still the same,
Handsomely nonchalant and
oh so tired
Of these skies that we cried and danced under
Diamond dew and delirious rage
Of the lavenders that grew on my skin

Your memories, that sink and surface
Like paper boats on flooded roads
How did you manage it?
Burrowed your way within my bones and made a home for
heartbreak
What curious shelter
Older but no wiser

Ghosts scarier than spirits that haunt me
Mine to love but not mine to keep
The raw meat of your rotten dreams and they devoured it
Weave me a gate to wonderland
For I can't paint it golden when it's not

Are you still the same,
Like the prisoner in the labyrinth of my daydreams,
Curiously careless and
oh so selfish

And so here I am,
Playing dead, hoping the killer passes right by
Hoping that someday, one day, I will be enough.

ALMOST

Blue times, take me in a snow globe
Cruel with your words, careless with your hands
Take me to the land of the flamingos
Terror and love seldom unlike

"Almost"
I almost left
And you almost forgave me
And it was almost a happy story

So go ahead
And mistake my cherry lips for lipstick
And the liquid eyes for mascara
The blue eyelid for colored shadow
My blushing cheeks for French rouge and not burning red
How awfully convenient

As tainted by sin as the artist who inflicted his prowess upon me
Your ivy heart and indigo mind
Held my gaze but tore my seams
And each night I stitch myself up
To smile and wave and laugh with the others
Unnoticed and ordinary, perfectly mundane
No sign of darkness, no sign of pain.

Bronze and Mahogany

UNTITLED

Give me sunrise,
Untethered, unbound
No trigger in black, a withered shack
Molten, frozen, blooming, bruised

Give me sunset,
Lowly, meek
Scarlet winter, placid seas

Give me storms,
Quiet still,
Raging battle, battered sins

I am the water,
The stone in its way
Tangled seasons, summer spray

Give me quiet, give me peace
Give me just one summer breeze
I am alive,
I am alive.

Bronze and Mahogany

15

TWILIGHT

can this twilight make something new of me
for if I live through the night make me an

ungovernable tide an unruly
beast that refuses to settle or bow

no more a dweller of what has been claimed
no longer confined to this skin that is

too small too thin too weak to keep me.
how boundless I could be, unlocked from the

margins the leeways the limits the rules
from the perimeters from the 'cannot's

perhaps I can bleed through my ends until
I am no more a stroke of Someone's brush

can this twilight make me into more than
a map a piece of paper too wrinkled

QUIET

Oh how bereaved that quiet rage,
Robbed of its form of speech,
Whose brightest dreams have nightly fled,
Beyond its earnest reach

Oh how suffocating, breathless,
To condense itself so slim
That not even light be let out
Such icy home its grim

Pity! The throne of regret
Born of disappointment and lies
Be not disappointed
And look up to the skies

The sapphire that shields
Its massive golden sphere,
Do yourself reveal,
And storm this quiet air

Oh quiet rage, be quiet no more
Learn to embrace the sound,
Howl through cemented shadows,
And leave cracks into the ground.

UNAPOLOGETIC

unapologetic and unwavering, I
have seen scarcely sorry souls lie
but the mountain for its span begs pardon not
and neither for its vastness the sky
so neither shall I
so neither shall I

SOLITARY

I sat ashore one tender dusk,
The sky mighty ablaze
The tears it shed were hugging me,
Burning me were its rays

And as the lungs of this dynamic globe
A single long breath drew,
My right hand so caressed my left
As though it had been you.

WOE

O that demure face does hide
Secrets buried in view of pride
Seem anxious brows that assay to mask
The red in eyes they cast aside

That pair of eyelids do plainly keep
Yearnings dry in bosom deep
Flickering lips that seem to forbid
Perching words a much-sought leap

Must those be twin shining eyes?
Or teary ones in distinct disguise
Whose tattered robe fools all but one
Unveiled to me those sorry sighs

Whose eyes were they, do you know?
Though the black beneath them did plainly show
Stygian circles of deflated days
Yet she spoke not of her woe

DAYLIGHT

Unbroken a sky sunk in the sand
A mind oceans have sewn
Alas, an anchored elegance
Never to be known

Stagnant waters, stagnant thoughts
Or a tranquil state of peace
Strung on threads of thin air
No prospect dare decease

Every cell and every tissue
A cosmos of wondrous shades
A nebula of howling beauty
Crimsons, violets and jades

Such a mind, embroidered with constellations
Glinting with beauty and shadow and no shame
It shan't e'er be anchored
Burning in immortal flame

Unbroken a sky sunk in the sand?
Perhaps daylight solidified,
A mind oceans have sewn,
Calm and calamity unified.

CHILDHOOD'S DAY

This giant, great expanse of sky
These olive blades that pass me by
The Earth as warm as its infancy
This sky, this Earth, they've cradled me

Laying down beside allies,
The bees, the birds, my tattered guise
Amidst the common summer spray
I drift away to childhood's day

Where life was held in light esteem
A new sun, a new dream
The mind impatient and restless so
Limbs that could not wait to grow

Alas, they did, the hands, the nose
As did the nights and shadows
Where was the sunshine, that bathes me now,
When drooped the daisies beneath my brow?

Though storms unnamed my mind had fought
Were they worth the dark the battle wrought?
Where is the child that screamed to the sky
With resolve, "I cannot, will not die!"

THE ROAD

I walked the path in silence
With Anger at my heel
Until she told me she was Sorrow
Trapped in all that I could feel

I walked the path in chatter
For Joy was walking with me
Until she told me she was Life
And how it was meant to be

I walked the path with Content
And she chatted all the way
And yet I came no wiser
Than I'd been the yester-day

I walked the path with Loss
And gravity was silenced by her hush
And yet by when I'd walked down the road
I'd never learnt so much.

WONDERS

To another millennia past,
I ask you not if Wonders have stayed
If due debts have been repaid
If sphinxes and mahals have decayed
If gold and silver are same still weighed

Instead I ask if men still put
One on a pedestal, one on his knees
Has humankind still not appeased?

Is love still known as right or wrong
Depending solely upon its form?
Do people still wish change their skin
Simply so they can belong?

Is still present a superior air,
Is still man above women there?
Is still a half in such despair,
Is still a dark? Is still a fair?

What dubious honor man must behold
And still seemingly worry of silver and gold

Is still a God spectator such?
Millenia past and yet no touch
How is the world still in His clutch,
I wonder not of Wonders much.

Bronze and Mahogany

14

TALK TO ME

O wanderer,
Why drown in sorrow's sea?
I'm right here, beside you
Come talk to me

O wanderer,
Why burn in your insecurities?
Turn the heat into your power
Come talk to me

O wanderer,
Must you jump and fall off the cliff of melancholy?
Oh, seek the light in the dark
Come talk to me

O wanderer,
Should you ever feel, you shall die of fatigue
Do remember, I'm there for you
Come talk to me

O wanderer,
Turn this rage, this anger, into ferocity
Should you ever want to talk
Come talk to me.

A BEAUTIFUL STORM

As I look at you,
I see a beautiful storm
And I wonder why you hold it in
Why to their whims you have conformed.

They tell you to keep building clouds,
Keep taking droplets in
And never let your thunder slash
And you just let them win

They want you to never let it go,
The weight of suspended rain
And you just let them sanction you
Over and over again

I wish I could show you
What I can see from backstage
How you could let it all out
If you only revealed your rage

They've grown you to learn that you simply can't raise a finger,
But they are your muscles and your bones
And only you control them,
For they are your own.

THE ELEGANT ART OF POETRY

A question heard by many,
A query still unsolved,
The elegant art of poetry,
What is it after all?

Many have said it expressing oneself,
But is that all it is?
Is that really all one writes to do,
To evince oneself in abyss?

That can't be all it is about
For then why, whenever one reads
One feels his garish mask come off
To words he does concede?

Why does one on reading feel,
The author is a friend
Why are they so relatable,
The words the poet penned?

Inexplicable it is, why on reading,
One just feels understood,
As if the poet wiped their tears
The way no other could.

ROSES AND DAISIES

We've all heard what they say,
Who'd pick a daisy in a field of roses?
Perhaps an artless Romeo may,
But artless nonetheless!

But why can't their 'artful' beings see,
That roses are full of thorns,
That they prick their buffs down to their knees,
Leaving them ruefully forlorn.

STARDUST

They think they know who I am
Just because they've seen me so
And if they countered my one weakness
They'd break me with a blow

They think they know me in and out
Like I am a simple thing
As if a single key could unlock
The door to my being

But they don't recognize, do they
That I am made of stardust
That I house a million mysteries
In me dwells the strongest gust

For I am home to sky-high peaks
And the wildest rivers you'd have seen
For I am an untamed ocean
And all the islands in between

They have no idea of me
Of the universe I hold inside
Of how I am the wings
Of every dream compelled to hide

So when next time you come
And you tell me I'm just not right
Allow me to enlighten you,
Darling, I'm infinite.

WOODS

When comes my time to say goodbye,
I will not weep, I will not cry
When I can count every breath on fingers mine
I will not cling, I will not pine

I shall sleep in peace, I shall lie down
And make my bed in leaves of brown
I shall embrace the world, for I,
I am not gone, I did not die

I am the air, the earth, the dust, the sea
I am the dew that sits on every leaf
I am the sunshine that's caught in eyes their
I am the rampant wind that ruffles strands of hair

Oh, when it's time for me to go to sleep
I shall not sob, I shall not weep
For I am not going, I never could
I could never escape these deep dark woods.

DREAMCATCHER

Frown upon my parched heart
Yet stay with me, never depart
Sing me a lullaby, and put me to sleep
O dreamcatcher, don't let me weep.

Braid into beauty my saltish tears
Ensnare forever my deepest fears
Stroke my hair into a slumber so sound
O dreamcatcher, lend me sleep profound.

Protect me from those nightmares, please
The monsters in my sleep, I cannot appease
Sing me a lullaby, and put me to sleep
O dreamcatcher, don't let me weep.

SNOW

You say I am just cold
Too cold for you to stay
And that if I don't melt the snow
You'll forever go away

But you don't see, even when I tell you to
That with patience you could see my spring
And my summer and fall and so much more
That my seasons together bring

And even if you couldn't
Isn't my snow enough for you?
For even my innermost glacier's white
Has only been seen by few.

STAR

Despair not, for you have not fallen
Just ricocheting in space, you are
What does it matter, if you're a shooting one
You're still a shining star.

JUNGLES

My mind is the thickest jungle
That you'd have ever seen
And you stand right at the edge
Looking for a path in between

But how can you expect me
To give you a way to arrive
When so many who've come before you
Have never let me thrive

The growing vines might make it seem
That I'm getting so much light
But my shrubs and bushes droop under
Hidden in everlasting night

So how can I let you in
Let you see my cold and dark
For I'm afraid your hand carries an axe
To chop off my shaky barks

Because I've lived under this canopy forever
So take it from me, for I know
It might be hard to enter
But it's a million times harder to go.

You

You think you are your clothes
Or the size you wear them in
Or the number that you see
On your weighing machine

You think you are your age
Or the length of your hair
You think the glasses on your eyes
Do your identity impair

When in fact you are your thoughts
And the words that you say
You're the songs that you hum
And the laughs you don't display

You're the genuine charming smile
That you have on when you awake
Or the snicker of satisfaction
When you successfully bake

You're all the books that've made you cry
And the people that you've loved
And the sweet morning sky
That you smile when you see above

You're all the things you've stood up for
And all the demons that you've fought
You're all the morals you're up to
Not the metrics that you're not.

SHARDS

I never believed people could break
Until I had your shards in my hand
And I wonder how you were so opaque
About all you had to withstand

I never knew that you were made of glass
Beautiful, yet bound to crack
And I never realized that, alas
Until you were so far gone, you couldn't come back.

BIRDSONG

Do not tell yourself you're odd
For you're the horizon of light and dark
You're the lone road, the journey
That no one's dared to embark

They tell me there's a heaven above
And if it's true, that the stars can see
Then they'd be proud immensely
Of what their atoms have come to be

They might call you strange and dotty
For dancing all day long
But perhaps that's because they're the ones
Who're deaf to the birdsong.

V

TIDE

Of course, they're willing to accept you
Just let go of who you are
Just completely change your identity
And behold, you are at par!

Their words form a tornado
They spin so fast at you
And if you give in to the storm
They might make you up anew

But take cover and shut them out
For you're stronger than their cyclone
Their attempts are feeble opposed to you
For you're so much more than blood and bone

You are the deepest ocean
Both untamed and vicious so
You're the wild and rampant sea
That has lived since ages ago

So whenever they try to shape you
The way they want you to be
Slip from their palms like water
And show them that you're free

Continued... Page 97

Bronze and Mahogany

For they should know how it's reckless
To mess with the ocean's peace
They should know how you're ferocious
How they just can't do you cease

So next time that they tell you
To keep it all inside
Let them know the hard way
That you can't command the tide.

LINGERING

What a waste
The angst, the wild that rest in those eyes
What a waste
The hours put in, waiting for dreams to actualize

What a waste
The dense weight of aims and visions and pursuits
What a waste
The tree of hope, when it's been sliced right from the roots

What a waste
Life, at its end, and she is lingering,
Long enough to touch just one drop of rain,
To feel some frozen ice again,
Before it all thaws into the drain...

A SHADOW

Please excuse my shaky voice
Or if my hands seem to tremble
For my reflection this morning
Was someone I didn't resemble

Nothing's really changed
It's all the same on the outside
But somehow it's no more an upside-down
But more of a down-upside

I see a stranger in the thousand mirrors
Like the night made me up anew
Like my limbs are just dragging a shadow
That time has forgotten too.

SPARKS

You gave me a spark, a fragile one
Thinking you'd just burn my skin
But you never knew the spark could turn
Into a fire I'd stifled within

The fire, it burned far and wide
It spread all throughout your town
You thought you could stop it from burning your mask
But this fire just won't die down

It'll burn down all your phony smiles
For it shall stay contained no more
It'll spread all through your icy lies
And show who you really were before

The fire, you cannot suppress it now
It's tired of being subdued
For even if it burns itself
At least it'll burn you too

Remember, it was you, after all
That did this fire start
But in the end, it's going to be
Exactly what tears you apart

You think you can do this fire control
But you're oblivious, you do not know
Your water's never been able to drown it
And neither will your snow.

WATERS

I can feel days getting shorter
And the darkness longing by
This seems the darkest night in autumn
A pitch-black daunting sky

I can touch the frost that's coming
Taste the winter on my tongue
Smell the snow from miles and miles
The cold air in my lungs

The chill, it has enveloped me
And reminisce, it makes me do
The nights spent in the winters
In sun shines and in blue

And I wish to float and swim
In the made-of-mist sea
And you can float in those waters too
If the waters call to thee.

GAZES

She gazes in the mirror all day long
From it validation she seeks
Not realizing she's being silly
For a mirror cannot speak.

It is 'beauty' she so dearly wants
And yet she doesn't know
That her charm and grace lie deeper within
While she waits for them to show.

UNSLEEPING

Wakeful,
Slumbers elude her nights
A frenzy of miscible blending thoughts,
She reeks of intoxication, drinking away the dusk
Falling awake,
Why must sleepless she remain?

STEADFAST

since that chilly night, you have not tried
to once write, you have not sought
one blue sky, you have not believed
in the mortality of this cold, unwavering expanse

when the world falls stone-cold
and the hard cement underfoot is glacial
you have not faith that perhaps
flowers bloom and bees hum and stars twinkle
oh so quietly

it seems all a paradox of daydreams,
warm skin and tender touches and spring
sunlight on a spiderweb, laughing through the tears

with the world- a castle of ice,
hell-bent on its barbaric ways and diabolical ordinances
with the world in a steadfast state of sin
you lost faith in a reality not bitter

but the sun does arise, and birds do sing
and spring will arrive
for no matter how cold or raw the snow is,
the sunshine shall not be contained
and neither shall you.

SIMPLE

'Simple' she seems
Too simple for them
'Dull' she appears
Like she is theirs to condemn

They have no clue of her
They couldn't if they tried
For she is a hidden current
A storm compelled to hide

Her mind is a hurricane
Of which they are wary
Her soul a story
No book's spine could carry.

WORDS

We are magicians playing tricks
Except not on a mystic hat
We dabble in words and wondrous mysteries
And perform stunts lies must combat

For every second that we live
Words gnaw inside our guts
And scratch and scream 'til we let them out
And let them breathe beyond our cuts

We listen to all that was never said
All the silences forever filled with dread
And we seek to spill them on parchment rough
The hushes of words that were never dead

Words these, they beg,
They claw at our very mind
And clamor for us to set them free
For they are creatures unconfined

For they contain in them the power
To bring back the deepest buried past
To make tears fall from the sternest eyes
And make nostalgia ever last.

TRY

You say you're afraid of countless things
Of creatures you haven't met
You say you're scared of catastrophes
That haven't occurred yet

You say you're scared of closed spaces
Where it seems in vacuum you drown
You say you're scared of going high
When you're really afraid of falling down

You say you're afraid of loneliness
But there's a difference between being lonely and alone
For it's sometimes solitude that makes you see
The beauty into which you've grown

You say you're afraid of the eerie dark
That it terrifies you, the night's cry
When you're really afraid of letting go of the light
And so you don't even care to try

But if there's one thing you'd hear from me
Let me tell you this
Just try once, to venture into the night
Let your skin by stars be kissed

Continued... Page 119

Try to once reach for the blue
That pulses in this sky
Try to once grab hold of all
That doesn't meet your eye

So just this once, hold onto life
But hold onto the tiny moments that lie
That lie between points in time
Oh just this once, try.

Bronze and Mahogany

ABOUT THE AUTHOR

Vaibhavi Pandey was born on the Christmas eve of 2005 in Secunderabad, India. Raised in Northern India in the 2000's, she started reading at early age, fascinated by the cheesy world of Geronimo and Thea Stilton. Soon enough she was 11 and reading fiction, fantasy and YA novels, as well as exploring the classics. Having had a literary interest for years, she started writing her own poetry, finding it a meaningful way to express herself, alongside classical dance. When she's not playing with her sister or studying in her room with headphones on (Taylor Swift, Queen, The Beatles!), you can find her either reading a good ol' YA book or writing yet another poem. Bronze and Mahogany is her debut, split into the sections '16', '15' and '14' signifying the age at which the poems were written.

Printed in Great Britain
by Amazon

87167529R00071